IMAGES
of England

WAKEFIELD

Westgate, Wakefield.

This view of Westgate shows its cabbies' shelter, the Great Bull Hotel and, on the left, the premises of the Wakefield & Barnsley Union Bank.

IMAGES
of England

WAKEFIELD

John Goodchild,
M. Univ.

TEMPUS

First published 1998
Reprinted 2001, 2003

Tempus Publishing Limited
The Mill, Brimscombe Port,
Stroud, Gloucestershire, GL5 2QG

British Library Cataloguing in Publication Data.
A catalogue record for this book is available from the British Library.

ISBN 0 7524 1196 9

Typesetting and origination by Tempus Publishing Limited
Printed in Great Britain by Midway Colour Print, Wiltshire

All of the illustrations used come from the authors Local History Study Centre.
This is open, free of charge, by prior appointment only. The author would be pleased to learn of other
photographs that readers have or know of.

The John Goodchild Collection, Below Central Library, Drury Lane, Wakefield, WF1 2DT. Tel: 298929.

A fascinating, timber-framed property in Marygate.

Contents

The Wakefield workhouse, in Park Lodge Lane. This workhouse was built for the Wakefield Union Board of Guardians and was opened in 1852; it replaced the old workhouse in George Street. The newer workhouse, in its turn, has recently been replaced with houses.

VIEW FROM WAKEFIELD PARK, WAKEFIELD.

Looking across Wakefield from the bandstand, which stood near the hilltop in Clarence Park. Nearby are the earthworks of Lawe Hill - an early medieval castle site of motte and bailey type.

Introduction

The ancient town of Wakefield lies between a crossing point of the River Calder and the crest of the northern side of its valley. The place is mentioned in the Domesday Book of 1086, when it was already the administrative centre of perhaps the largest manor in England. The Manor of Wakefield stretched from Normanton, in the east, up to the headwaters of the Calder and Holme rivers, in the west. In later times the town was also recognised as the administrative capital of the whole of the West Riding of Yorkshire. Here developed that county's prison, offices, lunatic asylum and registry of deeds and, from 1889, its County Council.

Wakefield was a self-administering borough from about 1190, it became a parliamentary borough (with one member) in 1832 and a modern municipal borough in 1848. It became a nominal city in 1888 (because Wakefield then became the head of a new diocese of the Church of England), and a county borough only in 1915. Wakefield became a part of the new metropolitan district, which took its name, in 1974.

The town has always been quite small. In the first national census of 1801 the population of the town itself was just over 8,000. Today the population of the enlarged area, which was the city of Wakefield until 1974, is just under 60,000. As an ancient market centre – its market was so ancient as to require no known market charter – Wakefield attracted the residents of the surrounding villages and small towns. Its shopkeepers, craftsmen and lawyers, as well as its market stall holders, greatly benefitted from this situation, as did its numerous innkeepers and other providers of popular entertainment.

Wakefield lay too at the meeting point of a number of highways, which were improved as turnpike or toll roads from the early 1740s. New road routes were added from the end of the eighteenth century. The town enjoyed the benefit of cheap transport, then only available by water, when weirs and locks were built in the River Calder up to the town, which were completed in or about 1702. Water transport was extended, upstream from Wakefield, from 1761 and ultimately over the Pennines, to the industrial North West, from 1804. A canal, running from the outskirts of Wakefield to Barnsley's coal fields, was opened from 1799. There were wagon and coaching services from the eighteenth century, steam-powered railways came in 1840, a horse bus service from the early 1890s, an electric tramway system in 1904 and subsequently motor bus services too. Wakefield's position on the, now electrified, main line from Leeds to London (the line was opened in 1866) makes its modern railway situation one of importance.

Transport improvements, combined with the availability of raw materials and facilities – especially coal and water power (both available locally) – aided the growth of the town's economy and general prosperity. Industry and commerce brought new employment openings and they, in turn, led to an increased population and a greater need for housing. However, the town did not begin to expand outside its medieval boundaries until the 1790s and not until far into the nineteenth century did housing begin its slow roadside development into the adjacent areas.

Textile processing and merchandising had existed here in medieval times, but it was the eighteenth century that saw the rise of numerous great Wakefield merchant princes. Textile factories only appeared, and then slowly, from the end of that century. The spinning of worsted yarn became a Wakefield speciality, along with various forms of specialist engineering work. The coal mining industry grew at an enormous rate around the town, only to decline finally in our own time. Women's employment was available on an increasing scale in the textile mills, from the mid-nineteenth century. Naturally the towns increased population, and those who lived in the nearby villages, demanded social, religious and educational facilities, which were provided on an ad hoc basis. Wakefield has become, in the last two decades, a major provider of evening entertainment, drawing young people to its discos from a very wide area.

The purpose of this book of photographs is to illustrate some of these aspects of the town's development. Naturally there are no photographs before the middle of the nineteenth century, when the process first became available. There are, unusually, no plans of the town, in detail, before the 1790s and very few engravings or paintings before that period either. The photographs used here date from the later nineteenth century and onwards.

John Goodchild, M.Univ
March 1998

An aerial view of the Lupset housing estate, *c.* 1930.

One

The Growth
of Wakefield

Central Wakefield, from the air in the 1920s, looking north. The medieval pattern of the town survives, with the ancient market area and the parish church being the focal points of roads leading from and to them.

The Bull Ring, before the opening of the electric tramways in 1904, from the bottom of Northgate and looking towards the cathedral. The buildings in the centre of the Bull Ring had been demolished in the 1890s.

Another early view from the air, in the 1920s, looking to the south.

Wakefield parish church became a cathedral in 1888. This shows that the outside of the building was recased, in new stone, starting from 1859. The tower and spire together are the tallest in Yorkshire and, along with the size of the church, mirror the prosperity and piety of medieval Wakefield.

Inside the cathedral, before the extension eastwards in the form of the Walsham How Memorial was added.

Wakefield's medieval castle, at Sandal. This was the stronghold of the great Manor of Wakefield, which stretched up to the Lancashire border, at the head of the valley of the Yorkshire Calder, and up the valley of the River Holme.

The ruins of Sandal Castle were used for a celebratory bonfire, for the coronation of Edward VII.

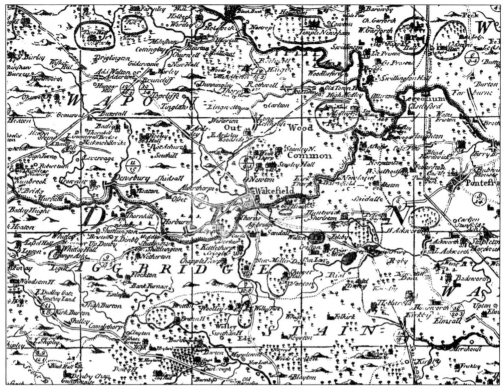

Wakefield and its vicinity in 1720.

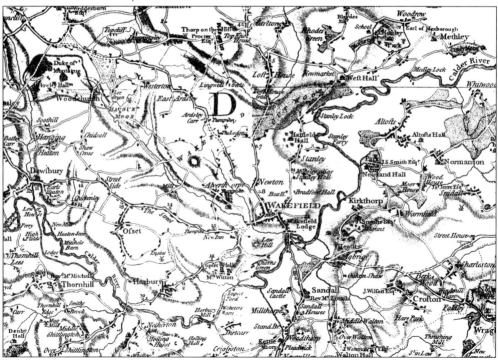

The vicinity of Wakefield, surveyed in 1767-70.

14

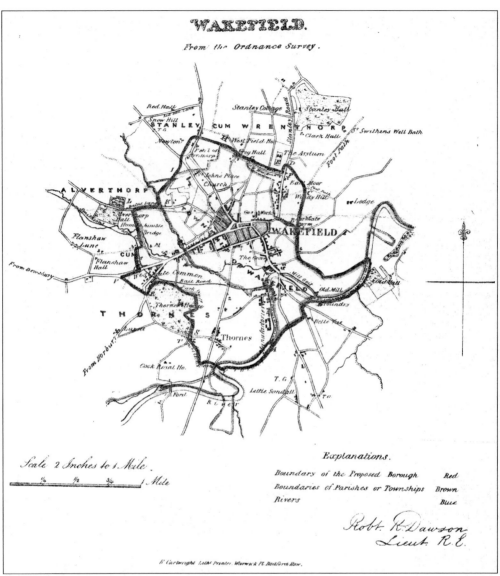

Wakefield in 1832; this was the new parliamentary borough.

These medieval buildings survived in the Cock & Swan Yard (later Bishopsgate), off Upper Westgate, until after the Second World War.

The Springs and the end of Warrengate. The watering place with its surrounding wall can be seen. The pinfold lay behind it.

Opposite: The Six Chimneys. This fine house was built in 1566 and again survived into the period of the Second World War.

A fine timber framed building, which stood at the top of Westgate until wantonly demolished after the Second World War.

A view of Wakefield from the town hall tower, looking east.

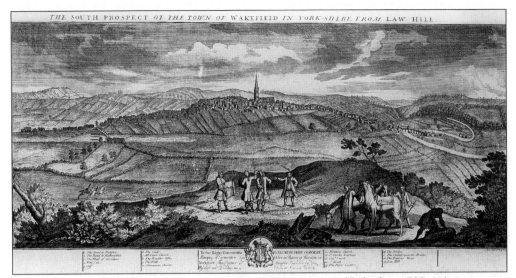

Wakefield on its hill, above the River Calder. This view was published in 1722.

Wakefield's Market Cross dated from the early eighteenth century. Despite public opposition, it was demolished in 1866. This is one of the earliest known photographs taken in the town.

Snapethorpe Hall was part of a medieval fortified establishment close to the road to Dewsbury. Its estate was purchased by the Corporation and the Lupset housing estate built upon it. The remains of the house stood until long after the Second World War.

Crazy Helen's Walk. This was part of the footway between Thornes and Wakefield, which was closed in the 1860s. The wall on the left was that of Thornes House's park. Both wall and footpath were destroyed by Wakefield Corporation after the Second World War. Middle Stone Age flints, similar to those found near the site of Sandal Castle, were discovered here.

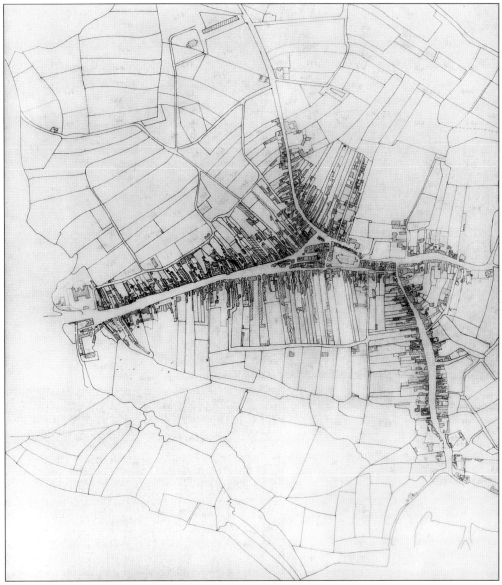

Wakefield's first large scale plan was drawn in the early 1790s. It shows the compact nature of the ancient town, bounded by its medieval back lanes.

A view from the air, in the 1920s, showing Wakefield's medieval bridge (twice widened in the eighteenth century), the weir and King's Mill nearby, the Chantry on the bridge and the adjoining industrial developments.

The Chantry chapel of St Mary the Virgin, on Wakefield Bridge, dated from 1356 and the immediately preceding years. It was demolished down to bridge footpath level and rebuilt, in 1847/48. The front was replaced by a third front after the Second World War. Note, on the right, the tower of Fernades Brewery and, on the left, the buildings of Clay's agricultural implements factory.

Wakefield Old Bridge, the Chantry chapel, the King's Mill and – beyond the Chantry – the great corn warehouse at Kirkgate station.

A new bridge across the River Calder was opened in 1933, between the site from which this photograph was taken and the old bridge.

The original front of the Chantry chapel was taken, in the late 1840s, to form, rebuilt, the front of a boathouse at Kettlethorpe Hall. The local authority's neglect of this important gem of medieval sculpture caused the whole to fall into complete ruin. Some of its stones have recently been placed in safe storage.

24

Two
Streets and Buildings

A narrow lower Northgate curves into the Bull Ring. The tramlines here ceased to be used in
1932, although the supports for their electric power wires can still be seen.

Upper Westgate, with Marygate to the left, and Little Westgate. On the left is the Church Institute of the 1860s.

Looking into the Bull Ring from the bottom of Wood Street and the top of Cross Square. Straight ahead is Union Street.

Lower Kirkgate. The Six Chimneys and the end of Legh Street are visible on the right.

Passengers were waiting in the Bull Ring, in 1949, to enter a centre-doorway bus, which would travel from Leeds to Sandal. These buses were painted red and followed the route of the erstwhile electric trams.

A view from the cathedral tower, in 1955, looking down on an enlarged Bull Ring and Northgate. The Stafford Arms Hotel is to the left of centre.

Slum clearance had left the site of the present bus station empty. Wakefield's celebratory end of war bonfire was held here in the mid-1940s.

A night-time view of the Bull Ring, from Union Street, after the Second World War. Vehicles are conspicuous solely by their absence.

Christmas lights in a pedestrianised Cross Square, in 1978.

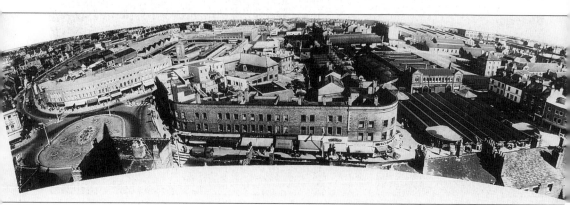

The changing face of central Wakefield. Humdrum architecture and wider streets replace the older, more intimate scale of the town centre.

The West Riding Court House, the town hall and Mechanics' Institute, in the 1890s.

The Music Saloon of the early 1820s, later to become the Mechanics' Institute and now the City Museum. Originally the Wakefield Dispensary (hospital) and baths were accommodated in its cellars.

The opening of the town hall, in 1880.

The town hall, in an empty Wood Street, 1890s.

The Public Baths, in Almshouse Lane, of the 1870s.

The County Hall opened in 1898 to house the new regional parliament - the West Riding County Council.

The West Riding Pauper Lunatic Asylum. This is now, for no apparent reason, called the Stanley Royd hospital. This, original, part of the asylum was opened in 1818. We see it here in 1979.

The old Grammar School at Wakefield, built in the 1590s.

The Grammar School and its associated buildings, on an engraving of c. 1820.

The present Grammar School's oldest building was erected in 1833/34 for the West Riding Proprietary School. It has been used by the Grammar School since the 1850s.

A Girls High School sports day, c. 1900. The school opened in 1878, in a house built around 1804 by J.P. Heywood, a wealthy barrister.

Wakefield's first hospital with beds lay at the corner of Lawefield Lane. The building, as shown here, originally had a further storey. It was known as the House of Recovery.

Clayton Hospital, *c.* 1900. The main buildings had been opened some two decades earlier.

The West Riding House of Correction (prison), at Wakefield, was opened here in the county town in the 1590s. As time passed and the population grew, it was necessarily enlarged and much of the present Wakefield gaol dates from the 1840s. That enlargement provided more accommodation than was required for the West Riding and part of the prison was let to the government – here we see their staff of the 1860s.

This is a group of the warder staff of the prison, between 1871 and 1882. The whole prison became government controlled in 1878.

The court house in Wood Street was used for county parliamentary elections. These are the (temporary) hustings at the election of 1848.

Almshouse Lane and some of the almshouses. These were founded in the mid-seventeenth century, by Cotton and William Horne, for poor women and men. The almshouses had been rebuilt in the late eighteenth century, into the form shown here. They were to be replaced, soon after 1900, by the present almshouses off Denby Dale Road.

Cliff Tree Wakefield

From a Sketch by G. Cope Esq.r 1826.
Etched by Emma Maria Stansfeld 1852.

The Cliff Tree at the top of Cliff Hill. General Wade's army is reputed to have camped here in connection with their putting down of the 1745 rebellion of Bonnie Prince Charlie.

Three
The Parks

Wakefield public park (Clarence Park), as it looked in its early days, in the 1890s. The Major Barker memorial fountain still stands, although Rose Cottage (shown here), the fine gate and the fencing have all now gone.

Clarence Park, again in its early days. One of the trees had been planted by the Duke of Clarence, one of Queen Victoria's many children, hence the name of the park.

The Pugneys Country Park is a recent amenity provided by Wakefield. Part of the site was a snad and gravel quarry and later coal was mined, before the park was created. This is how the park site looked in 1978.

Four
Changing Housing

Lower Northgate, with cleared shops and yards on the left, above Providence Street. A whole warren of yards filled this area; they were picturesque in their way, but had been much neglected.

The backs of houses in York Street. Some of these properties had been substantial and superior houses in their day.

Twins Place, Thornes Lane, with the 99 Arches beyond. This is a typical example of unplanned development in the nineteenth century.

Bank Street, off West gate. Houses of various periods are being demolished in front of the Drill Hall. Note the old woolstapler's warehouse behind the hall.

Georgian housing, in Northgate. The house with the pediment and bays was apparently built for Sir Thomas Blackett of Bretton Hall, possibly for a lady friend of his, in the 1780s.

The St John's housing-cum-church development, begun in 1791, seems to have been one of the first (if not the first) planned, new town developments of post-medieval England. It was divided from the nearest buildings, at that time, of the old town of Wakefield by some half a mile of open countryside.

The 1790s also saw the building of South Parade for the wealthy citizens of Wakefield. Unlike St Johns, it was not a development with a uniform series of façades.

Stoneleigh Terrace was developed, at the end of the nineteenth century, by a firm of quarry owners and stone merchants - the Seals. The long-widowed mother of George Gissing, the novelist, lived here for a time in its early history. The whole of the property is now used as a hotel.

The Elizabethan Heath Hall, built probably to the design of an architect of national fame, has had a chequered history. After occupation in the Second World War, by the military, it became increasingly derelict, until largely demolished – though not completely. Its internal timbers were in an impossible condition.

This is the delightful, early eighteenth century, Kettlethorpe Hall. A housing estate was built nearby and the Hall was used as a residential home. It was eventually rescued, converted and used privately once more - now as two family homes.

Holmefield, now a public house and hotel, was built in stages, from 1833, to be a gentleman's mansion. Holmefield Park, along with the adjacent Thornes House and its park, were bought by Wakefield Corporation immediately after the First World War. For a long time the house accommodated the Wakefield Museum.

Five
Shops and Industry

The garden of Mr and Mrs William Leatham, at Heath. This picture is from the time of Mrs Leatham's widowhood, probably in the 1860s. Various members of the Leatham family were bankers in Wakefield and Pontefract.

Chevet Hall, demolished in the 1950s, was part late medieval and part Georgian mansion. It was the home, from the 1750s, of the Pilkington family, baronets. Their parkland lake, Newmillerdam, was originally constructed to provide a water supply for Newmillerdam Mill. It was purchased by Wakefield Corporation and is now a delightful and well used country park.

The garden front of Chevet Hall.

Walton Hall has a most unusual and arresting setting – the Hall stands on a small island in a large lake. It dates, in its present form, from the 1760s and was built by the father of the world-famous naturalist Charles (Squire) Waterton, who died in 1865. The Hall is now used as a hotel which offers many recreational facilities.

The grave of Squire Waterton, at the head of the Walton Hall lake. At Walton Hall, Waterton introduced the idea of a nature sanctuary to the international community.

This building in Tammy Hall Street, was not a house but rather a plain woolstapler's warehouse before being altered to form prestigious lawyers offices early in the 1840s.

Newmillerdam, with the Dam Inn and Hilltop beyond and the almshouses just to the left of the inn, 1890s.

Newmillerdam, the mill (in the centre of the picture) and the overflow weir and control mechanism are all pictured here.

Lewis Hughes' shop in the Bull Ring, Wakefield. They enjoyed a well deserved reputation for old fashioned courtesy and personal service.

The corner shop. This is William Clark's stores in Carlton Street, Lawefield Lane.

The Borough Market and Market Hall, established here on what had been part of the Rectory House estate early in the 1850s.

Parkinsons motorcycle shop, 1920s.

A view of the whole town from the air, in the 1930s. This shows the town before piecemeal clearance for redevelopment ruined much of its ancient form.

The great Cattle Market was once the greatest in the north of England. It was established in 1765 and survived until after the Second World War.

The King's Mill at Wakefield Bridge End. Established in early medieval times, the mills were rebuilt on many occasions. They continued to use water power until demolished early in the 1930s to make way for the New Bridge, which was opened in 1933.

The mill wheel of Wakefield Upper Mill – a typical undershot, river-powered wheel, it still survives today.

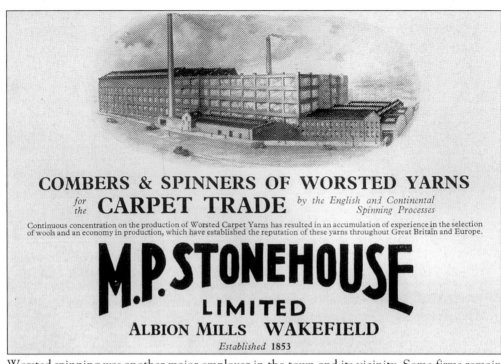

COMBERS & SPINNERS OF WORSTED YARNS
for CARPET TRADE *the* *by the English and Continental Spinning Processes*

Continuous concentration on the production of Worsted Carpet Yarns has resulted in an accumulation of experience in the selection of wools and an economy in production, which have established the reputation of these yarns throughout Great Britain and Europe.

M.P. STONEHOUSE
LIMITED
ALBION MILLS WAKEFIELD
Established 1853

Worsted spinning was another major employer in the town and its vicinity. Some firms remain today. M.P. Stonehouse's mills were in operation from the early 1850s to the mid-1990s.

The smoke from mills, collieries, engineering and other works, combined with domestic smoke, once covered Wakefield with an almost permanent pall. This engine, built in 1912 and used until 1974, was in service at Alverthorpe Mills.

Flanshaw New Mill of about 1808. Note the integral mill office, with its bay window. Originally woollen yarn was produced here.

Cheapside was a unique street of early nineteenth-century woolstaplers' warehouses. This view looks towards Westgate. Now the buildings have been put to a variety of new uses.

This was the largest of all the Wakefield woolstaplers' warehouses. It was situated in King Street. It was here that the young Titus Salt, later to be a great and famous industrialist, was apprenticed, to learn the raw wool trade, to Joseph Jackson. The brick building has been rendered and is now used as office premises.

Coal has been worked in the area since at least Roman times, but it was the opening of much wider markets, resulting from the development of a waterway system and subsequently a railway system, which caused the industry to develop. This was old Roundwood Colliery, its own private branch railway is shown crossing Dewsbury Road in the foreground.

Peggy Tub Main, in Denby Dale Road. This was one of the many small mines, which were operated alongside the larger ones.

Some colliers accommodation was built in Wakefield. This typical Long Row at Nostell, seen in 1976, survived longer than much housing of that type.

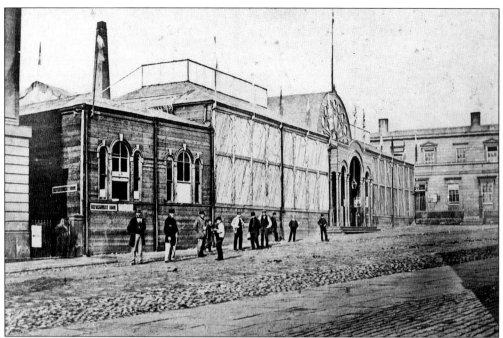

This temporary building housed Wakefield's Industrial and Fine Art Exhibition of 1865, the profit from which went to found what is now the Wakefield College. The building stood on the site of the present town hall. This photograph is perhaps the earliest dateable one of Wakefield, although photography here had been in use since 1849.

The Wakefield power station replaced the Corporation's electricity works of the 1890s. Its twin towers were eventually demolished in the 1990s. The travellers' encampment area is in the foreground.

Six
Pubs

A motorcycle gathering outside the Graziers Hotel, at the bottom of Market Street.

The Boy & Barrel Hotel, which, along with other buildings, occupied the Bull Ring until the late 1890s.

The inn at Thornes has an unusual dedication to Bishop Blaize, the patron saint of woolcombers. The original arch of the Lancashire & Yorkshire Railway and Thornes pump, on its original site, appear in the background.

The Three Houses Inn, at Sandal. Although now much gentrified, the buildings can still be recognised today.

The old Three Houses, at Sandal. This is the inn where Nevison the highwayman was arrested in the 1680s. He was ultimately executed.

The Strafford Arms Hotel, in the Bull Ring at Wakefield. This was a fine, spacious hotel, which, until the coming of railways, had been one of Wakefield's principal coaching inns. As Wakefield stood at the junction of various major road routes, its coaching activity was considerable.

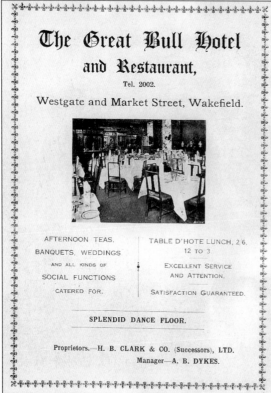

The Great Bull Hotel and Restaurant,

Tel. 2002.

Westgate and Market Street, Wakefield.

AFTERNOON TEAS.
BANQUETS, WEDDINGS
AND ALL KINDS OF
SOCIAL FUNCTIONS
CATERED FOR.

TABLE D'HOTE LUNCH, 2 6,
12 TO 3

EXCELLENT SERVICE
AND ATTENTION.

SATISFACTION GUARANTEED.

SPLENDID DANCE FLOOR.

Proprietors.—H. B. CLARK & CO. (Successors), LTD.
Manager—A. B. DYKES.

The Great Bull, at the top of Westgate. It was situated in the area known as the Corn Market and was rebuilt in its present form early in the 1770s. The hotel possessed a large number of bedrooms. This is an advertisement from the 1930s.

Seven

Chapels and Churches

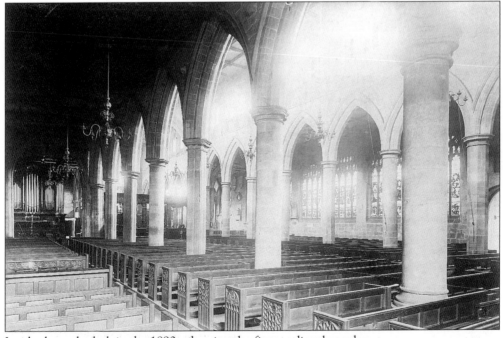

Inside the cathedral, in the 1890s, showing the fine medieval arcades.

The chancel of the cathedral, with the bishops's throne on the right. The stonework here is also of medieval date. However, early in the twentieth century the building of the Walsham How memorial extension completely altered the appearance of its eastern end.

Nonconformity can be traced in Wakefield back into the early 1500s. The first purpose-built chapel was opened in 1697. It was replaced by Westgate chapel in 1751/52. This is a view looking down the chapel yard in the mid-nineteenth century, with the chapel parsonage of 1804/05 on the left. In its last years the premises were used as an hotel. It was demolished after the Second World War.

The interior of Westgate chapel, opened in 1752, before alterations were completed in 1882. Much of the woodwork in the chapel today dates from the earlier building of 1697.

Wakefield's second church, St John's, was consecrated in 1795. Like the earlier Westgate chapel, there are burial catacombs below it.

St Mary's, Primrose Hill. This church was built, in the 1850s, in a working class area close to Kirkgate station.

Christ Church, Thornes Lane. This church was built, in the 1870s, to serve another working class area - of boatmen's families, maltsters and the like.

ST. ANDREW'S HALL, WAKEFIELD.
First Portion Opened September 8th, 1906, by
LADY ST. OSWALD.

A. G. WHALEY, Vicar.

St Andrew's church, Peterson Road, was built in the 1840s. Again this church was opened to serve a working class area but, unlike St Mary's and Christ Church, it survives. Its extensive church hall premises were opened, in 1906, near to the church.

The chapels (Nonconformist and Church of England) in the Borough Cemetery, opened in 1859. The large monument was one of the earliest, as well as by far the largest, ever erected in the cemetery. It commemorates William Shaw, a wealthy railway contractor of Stanley Hall. He died in 1859 and is interred in the Nonconformists' section of the cemetery.

The Baptist chapel of the mid-1840s in Fair Ground Road, now George Street. This is a plain building, though it has an ornate and impressive façade.

The interior of the Zion Congregational chapel in George Street. This was rebuilt in the 1840s on the same site used since the early 1780s.

Eight

Transport

The main road system of Wakefield became at various dates from 1741 run by turnpike and toll-taking trusts and continued so until the latter were abolished early in the 1880s. Pictured are the bar and barhouse, on the Aberford turnpike from Wakefield, near the top of Stanley Hill.

Agbrigg Barhouse. This was situated on the Wakefield & Weeland turnpike road (now Doncaster Road), at the bottom of Heath Common.

Barnsley & Grange Moor
TURNPIKE-ROAD.

TABLE OF
TOLLS

TO BE TAKEN AT THE
Barnsley, Bretton Mill New Bar, and Flockton Bar.

	s.	d.
For every Horse or other Beast, drawing any Coach, Stage Coach, Berlin, Landau, Barouche, Chariot, Chaise, Chaise Marine, Chair, Curricle, Phæton, Calash, Sociable, Car, Gig, Caravan, Van, Hearse or Litter, the Sum of	0	8
For every Horse or other Beast, drawing any Waggon or other such Four-wheeled Carriage, or any Cart or other such Two-wheeled Carriage, the following Tolls, viz.:		
For every Horse or other Beast, drawing any such Waggon or other Carriage, having the Fellies of the Wheels thereof of the Breadth of Six Inches and upwards, the Sum of	0	5
For every Horse or other Beast, drawing any such Waggon or other Carriage, having the Fellies of the Wheels thereof of the Breadth of Four Inches and a Half, and under Six Inches, the Sum of	0	6
For every Horse or other Beast, drawing any such Waggon or other Carriage, having the Fellies of the Wheels thereof under the Breadth of Four Inches and a Half, the Sum of	0	7½

A table of tolls charged on the local Barnsley to Grange Moor turnpike.

The horse remained the primary source of transport until the time of the First World War. These fine horses are apparently showing in Clarence Park, in Wakefield.

An early Wakefield motoring group.

This three-wheeler stands outside a house in South Parade.

Riverbed cobblestones, from the roadway behind the Opera House.

Yorkshire setts and flags form the roadway in a yard off Westgate.

Kirkgate station was opened in 1840, but replaced in the 1850s by the present handsome building. Until 1866 it was Wakefield's only railway station: from here one caught trains for London as well as for the east, west and north.

The Kirkgate railway viaduct was opened in 1840. The promotion for the building of this viaduct caused a great amount of trouble. It was argued that the street should be passed by one arch, rather than the planned three. One arch is used today.

The so-called Ninety-Nine Arches. In fact there are probably only ninety-five of them. Some of these were in use from 1857, the remainder from 1866.

A horse bus, at the bottom part of Northgate, opposite the cathedral tower. The narrow entrance to Cross Square can be seen - this was only opened out in the first decade of the present century.

Two trams for Leeds, standing at the Sandal terminus, close to the Castle Inn. The trams ran between Sandal and Leeds and between Agbrigg and Ossett, from 1904 to 1932.

An early West Riding passenger vehicle.

A bus passes through floodwaters in Denby Dale Road.

The Wakefield bus station on a wet
day in 1978.

A view looking north towards Wakefield in 1949. On the left are the Belle Vue locomotive sheds, on the right a few boats remain on the Barnsley Canal. The central field was to become the site of the new power station. The River Calder crosses the picture.

A view similar to the previous one in its coverage, but this time looking south. The Corporation's sewerage works are in the foreground and Heath Common is in the background, on the left.

Thornes Lane, seen from near its junction with Ings Road. The great corn elevator (used to lift grain from boats) passes over the road.

Thornes Lane, seen from the end of Mark Lane. In the centre of the picture are the gateways through which railway wagons passed, going to and from the canal transhipment point. In the foreground Smithson's railroad passed by, it was opened to bring coal to the boats in 1798.

The Wakefield waterfront after the Second World War; commercial traffic had almost ceased at this time.

Wakefield waterfront's southern side, with warehouses and maltings but no working traffic. Left of centre is the great 1790s warehouse of the Calder & Hebble Navigation, beyond this is the earlier warehouse of the same company - at the top of Fall Ing Cut.

A little traffic on the Calder & Hebble Navigation in Wakefield pond, *c.* 1956.

The skeletal remains of the electric tramway company's staithing. This carried a crane that unloaded coal from boats, to be used in their adjoining generating station.

A further view from the air, in the 1920s, with more working boats in evidence. Wakefield Old Bridge is in the right foreground.

An advertisement by Reynolds & Haslegrave of Wakefield, corn millers, showing their two King's and West Riding mills – and their road traction engine at work, c. 1900.

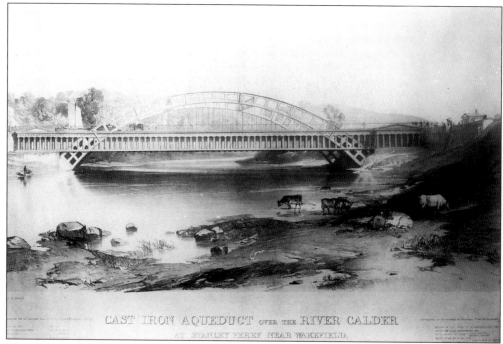

CAST IRON AQUEDUCT over the RIVER CALDER
AT STANLEY FERRY NEAR WAKEFIELD.

The Aire and Calder Navigation first brought boats upstream to Wakefield in about 1702, following the meanderings of the River Calder by the use of weirs and locks. This circuitous route was, in part, bypassed in 1839 when a new canal, and this splendid aqueduct at Stanley Ferry, were both opened by a seagoing schooner built at Wakefield.

Fall Ing Cut was opened in 1761 to bring boats for the first time into Wakefield Mill Dam – Wakefield Pond as the boatmen called it. The new cut passed below both the Doncaster and Barnsley roads and the original bridges were much lower – they were raised to allow for the passage of seagoing vessels in about 1840. The building on the extreme left was the warehouse of the Huddersfield (narrow) Canal Company, completed in the early 1820s.

Steamers used the Wakefield waterway system. Here one tows an equally well loaded dumb boat upstream, past the corner of the present bus depot.

The Calder & Hebble Navigation's lockhouse and lock cabin, at the foot of Broad Cut at Calder Grove. The buildings have been replaced with a modern lockhouse.

The entrance lock, at Heath, to the Barnsley Canal. The toll office and stables, for towing horses, can be seen on the left, *c.* 1900.

The top lockhouse and lock, near the top of the Walton flight on the Barnsley Canal, with Walton Hall park beyond.

Horses were used for towing on the Barnsley Canal at Heath. The boat is approaching the bridge carrying Doncaster Road.

A walk along the Barnsley Canal's tow path, through the Walton cutting.

Nine

Employment and Workers

Industrial development in the shape of engineering and textiles works, at the bottom of
Alverthorpe Road, c. 1930.

Rural industry is shown here with Coxley Mill and its cloth tenters and workers' cottages. The mill was opened in the 1780s.

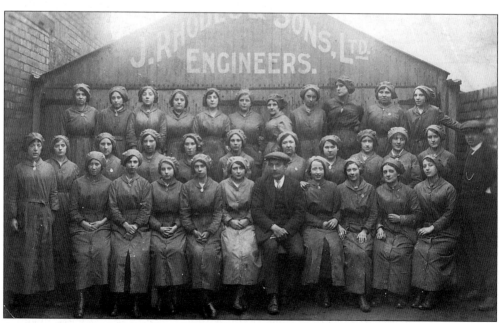

A group of female workers at Joseph Rhodes engineering works, at Belle Vue.

Ten
Life in Wakefield

Sandal developed, from the end of the nineteenth century, as a desirable residential suburb of Wakefield for the middle class. These are villas in Agbrigg Road, close to Sandal station.

This farm and the Jolly Sailor inn (the latter since rebuilt and renamed), were situated at the bottom of Heath Common.

Flooding was a common occurrence in the lower parts of the town. This is a flooded Westgate Common, in 1922.

A horse bus company's omnibus service, introduced early in the 1890s, allowed workers to live outside the town centre. This is one of the buses at Outwood in their last years of service – the immediate success of the electric tramway caused the liquidation of the bus company in 1905.

Alverthorpe station. Suburban railway services also helped ribbon development, as a result of workers being able to live away from the immediate area of their work.

Branches of the early chain stores, owned by non-local firms, slowly spread into the area – Boots the chemist is a classic example.

The Springs, before widening was undertaken after the Second World War.

The rural Manygates Lane, c. 1900.
This was the old route of the main
road to Barnsley.

The club house of the Heath Common golf course. This was built by a company formed expressly for that purpose.

The new Wakefield golf house at Woodthorpe. The course supplemented and ultimately replaced the Heath Common course.

Coxley Valley was a well used recreational facility. Many Sunday School groups enjoyed outings there. A café and swings were among the diversions offered.

This display formed part of the celebrations for the coronation of George VI and the present Queen Mother, in 1937.

Royalty visited Wakefield but seldom. However, early in their reign, the town enjoyed a visit by George V and Queen Mary, pictured here at the Cradocks' ropeworks in Denby Dale Road.

A procession in Market Street – possibly marking Whitsuntide. On the left is the gate to Carters Brewery and, on the right, are the United Methodist chapel and the post office.

This parade of horses with vehicles probably took place in Clarence Park.

A coronation party in 1953, believed to be in Charles Avenue.

Clarence Park. A group of children enjoy this urban lung.

The Scout troop of Holy Trinity church, George Street.

Eleven

Around the Town

Belle-Vue, Wakefield.

Doncaster Road, Belle Vue. This is a mixture of old and new buildings, shops and the borough cemetery (on the right).

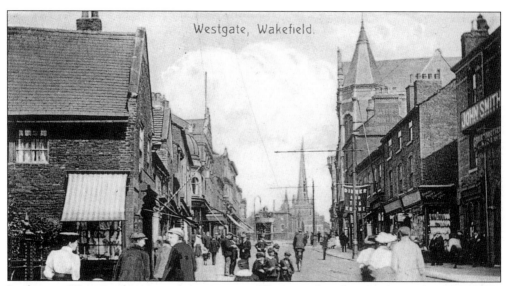

Looking up Westgate from near the entrance to Westgate chapel.

The top of Westgate, showing the Corn Market, with the old (*c.* 1820) Corn Exchange in the centre and the new (1838) Corn Exchange on the right, before the tramways arrived in 1904.

The Bull Ring with its new complex of tramlines and a new statue of Queen Victoria.

An early covered tram approaches the top of Westgate.

Looking down Westgate, with the Co-op's Unity Hall on the left and the Opera House on the right.

This town centre shop had most ornate window layouts.

A further Bull Ring view, looking to the end of Westmoreland Street.

A narrow Upper Kirkgate, looking towards the cathedral.

Westgate in later tramway days, with the 1860s Church Institute on the left.

Upper Westgate, with a line of horse-drawn cabs in front of the Old Corn Exchange.

Westgate, below the railway bridge. There are trees growing in the carriageway and timber framed buildings can be seen in the centre.

The Stork Gates (a stork being the crest of the Gaskell family of Thornes House) in Thornes Road, before the park was bought by the Corporation in 1919.

As well as having an aqueduct, Stanley Ferry had also a wooden toll bridge, built in the 1870s to replace the actual Stanley Ferry.

Drift coal mines were a common sight in the vicinity of Wakefield.

Not frequently seen by the general public were colliers having their break and snap underground.

Twelve

Villages Nearby

The tram terminus at Sandal, with the Castle Inn on the right.

Entering Sandal village from Wakefield.

En route to Sandal.

The Georgian chapel, in Bretton Park.

Bretton Hall, seen across the lower lake.

Woolley Hall with its ornamental gardens.

Woolley Dam, situated close to the Wakefield to Barnsley Road.

A scene in Crofton.

The Balk at Walton.

Sharleston Hall's gazebo is seen to the left, along with one of the pigeon cotes and fine entrance pillars.

Sharlston Hall, a medieval building with a fine doorway dating from the sixteenth century.

Normanton's medieval church – one of a number of such churches in the Wakefield area.

Workaday Normanton. High Street shops are pictured and a tramcar makes its way down the street.

Heath Common. Cobbler's Hall (right of centre) was an eighteenth-century school, which attracted pupils from far and wide - even from the North American colonies.

The White House, at Heath – this was the last thatched house in the whole area.

Kirkthorpe village. The Cold Bath is visible, to the right of centre.

Kirkthorpe. Shown here are John Freeston's almshouses for poor men, which were built in the 1590s.

Drury Lane, in rural Altofts.

The Aberford Road at Lake Lock, Stanley.

Alverthorpe Hall, a fine though relatively small mansion, set on the outskirts of Wakefield.

The great snow of 1906, on the road between Wakefield and Horbury. The tramlines are apparently being cleared.

The lodge and entrance to Outwood Hall. The park, formerly attached to the Hall, is now largely occupied by a housing estate. However, the stable block survived the demolition of the Hall.

The village of Wrenthorpe or Potoil – the latter (unofficial) name derived from the pottery kilns which survived there into the eighteenth century.

040 Lee Fair,

Lee Fair, West Ardsley. This was the site of an ancient horse fair which survives today.

Free Library and Council Offices, Horbury.

Horbury, like so many local communities, was self-administered until 1974, at which time it became a part of the new Wakefield Metropolitan District. Pictured are its town hall and public library.

The ford of Horbury Junction - across the River Calder.

The toll bar house on the right, at Horbury Bridge, was rebuilt in a garden at Netherton. The older bar house can just be seen behind it; it dates from the time (pre c. 1830) when the turnpike road went up Sandy Lane. The Midland Railway viaduct, constructed in the early twentieth century, passes over the road. Through it can be seen the elegant frontage of the Bingley Arms Inn.